The Gregorian and Julian calendars: wherein are taught how to find arithmetically the leap-years, golden number, epacts, dominical letters, Easter Day, the moon's age, ... To which is now added, Memorial verses, ... By Aaron Hawkins.

Aaron Hawkins

ECCO

PRINT EDITIONS

Eighteenth Century
Collections Online
Print Editions

Gale ECCO Print Editions

Relive history with *Eighteenth Century Collections Online*, now available in print for the independent historian and collector. This series includes the most significant English-language and foreign-language works printed in Great Britain during the eighteenth century, and is organized in seven different subject areas including literature and language; medicine, science, and technology; and religion and philosophy. The collection also includes thousands of important works from the Americas.

The eighteenth century has been called "The Age of Enlightenment." It was a period of rapid advance in print culture and publishing, in world exploration, and in the rapid growth of science and technology – all of which had a profound impact on the political and cultural landscape. At the end of the century the American Revolution, French Revolution and Industrial Revolution, perhaps three of the most significant events in modern history, set in motion developments that eventually dominated world political, economic, and social life.

In a groundbreaking effort, Gale initiated a revolution of its own: digitization of epic proportions to preserve these invaluable works in the largest online archive of its kind. Contributions from major world libraries constitute over 175,000 original printed works. Scanned images of the actual pages, rather than transcriptions, recreate the works *as they first appeared.*

Now for the first time, these high-quality digital scans of original works are available via print-on-demand, making them readily accessible to libraries, students, independent scholars, and readers of all ages.

For our initial release we have created seven robust collections to form one the world's most comprehensive catalogs of 18th century works.

Initial Gale ECCO Print Editions collections include:

History and Geography
Rich in titles on English life and social history, this collection spans the world as it was known to eighteenth-century historians and explorers. Titles include a wealth of travel accounts and diaries, histories of nations from throughout the world, and maps and charts of a world that was still being discovered. Students of the War of American Independence will find fascinating accounts from the British side of conflict.

Social Science

Delve into what it was like to live during the eighteenth century by reading the first-hand accounts of everyday people, including city dwellers and farmers, businessmen and bankers, artisans and merchants, artists and their patrons, politicians and their constituents. Original texts make the American, French, and Industrial revolutions vividly contemporary.

Medicine, Science and Technology

Medical theory and practice of the 1700s developed rapidly, as is evidenced by the extensive collection, which includes descriptions of diseases, their conditions, and treatments. Books on science and technology, agriculture, military technology, natural philosophy, even cookbooks, are all contained here.

Literature and Language

Western literary study flows out of eighteenth-century works by Alexander Pope, Daniel Defoe, Henry Fielding, Frances Burney, Denis Diderot, Johann Gottfried Herder, Johann Wolfgang von Goethe, and others. Experience the birth of the modern novel, or compare the development of language using dictionaries and grammar discourses.

Religion and Philosophy

The Age of Enlightenment profoundly enriched religious and philosophical understanding and continues to influence present-day thinking. Works collected here include masterpieces by David Hume, Immanuel Kant, and Jean-Jacques Rousseau, as well as religious sermons and moral debates on the issues of the day, such as the slave trade. The Age of Reason saw conflict between Protestantism and Catholicism transformed into one between faith and logic -- a debate that continues in the twenty-first century.

Law and Reference

This collection reveals the history of English common law and Empire law in a vastly changing world of British expansion. Dominating the legal field is the *Commentaries of the Law of England* by Sir William Blackstone, which first appeared in 1765. Reference works such as almanacs and catalogues continue to educate us by revealing the day-to-day workings of society.

Fine Arts

The eighteenth-century fascination with Greek and Roman antiquity followed the systematic excavation of the ruins at Pompeii and Herculaneum in southern Italy; and after 1750 a neoclassical style dominated all artistic fields. The titles here trace developments in mostly English-language works on painting, sculpture, architecture, music, theater, and other disciplines. Instructional works on musical instruments, catalogs of art objects, comic operas, and more are also included.

The BiblioLife Network

This project was made possible in part by the BiblioLife Network (BLN), a project aimed at addressing some of the huge challenges facing book preservationists around the world. The BLN includes libraries, library networks, archives, subject matter experts, online communities and library service providers. We believe every book ever published should be available as a high-quality print reproduction; printed on-demand anywhere in the world. This insures the ongoing accessibility of the content and helps generate sustainable revenue for the libraries and organizations that work to preserve these important materials.

The following book is in the "public domain" and represents an authentic reproduction of the text as printed by the original publisher. While we have attempted to accurately maintain the integrity of the original work, there are sometimes problems with the original work or the micro-film from which the books were digitized. This can result in minor errors in reproduction. Possible imperfections include missing and blurred pages, poor pictures, markings and other reproduction issues beyond our control. Because this work is culturally important, we have made it available as part of our commitment to protecting, preserving, and promoting the world's literature.

GUIDE TO FOLD-OUTS MAPS and OVERSIZED IMAGES

The book you are reading was digitized from microfilm captured over the past thirty to forty years. Years after the creation of the original microfilm, the book was converted to digital files and made available in an online database.

In an online database, page images do not need to conform to the size restrictions found in a printed book. When converting these images back into a printed bound book, the page sizes are standardized in ways that maintain the detail of the original. For large images, such as fold-out maps, the original page image is split into two or more pages

Guidelines used to determine how to split the page image follows:

• Some images are split vertically; large images require vertical and horizontal splits.
• For horizontal splits, the content is split left to right.
• For vertical splits, the content is split from top to bottom.
• For both vertical and horizontal splits, the image is processed from top left to bottom right.

THE
Gregorian and *Julian*
CALENDARS:

Wherein are Taught

How to find Arithmetically the Leap-Years,
Golden Number, Epacts, Dominical Letters.
Easter Day, the Moon's Age, the Moon's
Southing, and the Times of High Water, in
both Accounts, for ever.

Together with an

EXPLANATION

OF THE

Roman Indiction, the *Julian* Period, and the
Calends, Nones and Ides, with every Thing suited to
the meanest Capacity, for understanding the NEW
CALENDAR; so that any Person being only ac-
quainted with Addition and Subtraction, may perform
most of the Rules, and have a perpetual ALMANACK
always in his Head, or at Hand.

To which is now added,

MEMORIAL VERSES,

Adapted to the *Gregorian* Account, or New Style,

In Imitation of Mr *Street*'s MEMORIAL VERSES for the
Julian Account, or Old Style

By AARON HAWKINS

The Law is good, 1 Tim chap 1 ver 8

LONDON

Printed for the AUTHOR, and Sold at his House
opposite *Scotch-Hall*, *Water-Lane*, *Black-Friars*, and
may be had of M. COOPER, in *Paternoster-Row*

M DCC LII.

(Price One Shilling and six-pence)

PREFACE.

SINCE the Reformation of the Calendar by Pope Gregory the XIIIth, Anno 1582. several Proposals have been made in his Majesty's Dominions, in order to reduce our Stile to the Gregorian, but to no Purpose; for the Proposers, most of them unable to bring their Proposals into Parliament, and others void of Truth, that none dare attempt it; but now it is thought will pass into a Law, according to the Bill which is in the Honourable House of Commons (it having already passed the House of Lords) and how can it be otherwise, when such Great and Learned Men have taken it in Hand, as the noble Earls of Chesterfield and Macclesfield, Martin Folks, Esq; President of the Royal Society, Dr. Bradley, his Majesty's Professor of Astronomy, and Mr. Duvall, Barrister in the Temple, all of them Stars of the first Magnitude in the Horizon of Truth.

But I shall not trouble my Reader with a long Preface, the Body of the Book not permitting it, only assure him, that the Rules in this small Treatise are reduced to the proposed Method for correcting the Calendar now in Use.

AARON HAWKINS.

CONTENTS.

THE
Gregorian and *Julian*
CALENDARS,
Arithmetically Explained.

CHAP. I.

Of the *Julian* Leap-Years.

THO' the Solar Year, or the Earth's Revolution in the Ecliptic, is about 365 Days 5 Hours 49 Minutes; yet we reckon only 365 Days (excepting in Leap-Year) omitting the 5 Hours 49 Minutes, which are but 11 Minutes fhort of 6 Hours, that it comes, that every common Year is about 6 Hours too fhort, which in four Years make almoft a Day, and that Day we add or put in, in, the Month of *February* in every 4th Year, which is ftiled the Biffextile Year, by reafon it contains 366 Days; now to know if the Year propofed is Biffextile or not.

B   The

The RULE.

Divide the Number of Years by 4, and if there is no Remainder, it's a Leap-Year, or a Year of 366 Days; but if 1, 2, or 3 remain, it is 1, 2, or 3 Years after Leap-Year, and those Years contain only 365 Days.

EXAMPLE I.

If the given Year is 1748, which divided by 4 gives 437 for the Quotient, and no remainder, which according to the Rule was a Leap-Year, or a Year of 366 Days.

EXAMPLE II.

Suppose the given Year to be 1751, which divided by 4, gives 437 for the Quotient, and 3 remaining, which according to the Rule is 3 Years after Leap-Year, and contains only 365 Days.

CHAP. II.

Of the Gregorian *Leap-Years.*

THE *Gregorian* Leap-Years is found after the same Manner as the *Julian*, only in the Hundredth Years, which was the Reason of the Reformation of the Calendar, *Anno* 1582, by Pope *Gregory* XIII. and is likely to produce the same Effect in his Majesty's Dominions.

If the Tropical Year was precisely 365 Days, 6 Hours, the *Julian* Stile had needed no Correction; but its Length according to Dr. *Halley*, is found to be 365 Days, 5 Hours, 48' 54" 41''' 27'''' 31''''' which is short of 365 Days, 6 Hours, by 11' 05" 18''' 32'''' 29''''' and this in 400 Years amounting

ing

ing to 3 Days 1 Hour 55' 23" 36''' 33'''' 20''''' fo that fince the General Council of *Nice*, *anno* 325, the Seafons of the Year have gone back 11 Days, and this Error is ftill increafing; fo that if the *Julian* Year goes on thus without any Correction, the Vernal or Spring Equinox, in about 9 or 10 Thoufand Years will be upon *Chriftmas* Day; how ftrangely will the Seafons of the Year be alter'd, to what they are now, if any People were to be alive to fee it! But if the World endure fo long, the People then living will not know any Alteration, becaufe this Alteration is made gradually, and by little and little, fo that in an Age the Vulgar cannot perceive it.

To prevent the like Retrogradation for the future, Pope *Gregory* XIII. *anno* 1581, iffued his Bull; ordering 1 That, in 1582, the 5th of *October* fhould be called the 15th and fo on. 2. The Aftronomical Tables and Obfervations of that Time making the Anticipation of the Equinox to be at the Rate of 3 Days in 400 Years, he ordered, that every 400 Years, 3 Days fhould be fuppreffed, by reckoning the grand Jubilees, or centenar Years 1700, 1800, 1900, which, in the *Julian* Calendar are Leap-Years, to be common Years of 365 Days. This Rule not taking place 'till 1700, becaufe the 10 Days already fuppreffed, exceeding the juft Quantity, including the Correction due from 1582 to 1700. And to know if the Hundredth Years are Leap-Years, or Common, take this

RULE.

Reject two Cyphers to the right Hand, and divide the remaining Figures or Cyphers by 4, and if nothing remain it is a Biffextile, but if any thing remain it is a common Year.

Ex-

EXAMPLE I.

To know if the Year 1800 is a Biſſextile or common Year, divide 18 by 4, and the Remainder is 2, which, according to the Rule, is a common Year.

EXAMPLE II.

To know if the Year 2000 is a Biſſextile or Common Year, divide 20 by 4, and there remains nothing, which, according to the Rule, is a Biſſextile Year, or a Year of 366 Years.

CHAP. III.

Of the Julian *and* Gregorian *Golden Numbers.*

THE Golden Number, or Cycle of the Moon, is alſo called the Metonic Cycle, called ſo from its Inventor *Meton*, and is a Period of 19 Years, which when they are compleated, the New Moons and Full Moons return on the ſame Days of the Month; ſo that on whatever Days the New and Full Moons fall this Year, 19 Years hence they will happen on the very ſame Days of the Month (though not at the ſame Hour) as *Meton*, and the Fathers of the Primitive Church thought; and therefore at the Time of the Council of *Nice*, when the Way of ſetting the Time for obſerving the Feaſt of *Eaſter* was eſtabliſhed, the Numbers of the Lunar Cycle were inſerted in the Calendar, which, upon the Account of their excellent Uſe, were ſet in Golden Letters, and the

the Year of that Cycle for any Year, was called the Golden Number of that Year, which how to find take the following

RULE.

Add one to the Year of our Lord, and divide by 19, the Remainder is the Golden Number, but if nothing remain the Golden Number is 19.

EXAMPLE I.

What will be the Golden Number for the Year 1753 ?

$$19)1754(92$$
$$44$$
$$6$$

I add one to the Year 1753, which makes 1754, and divide by 19, the Remainder 6 is the Golden Number.

EXAMPLE II.

What will be the Golden Number for the Year 1792 ?

$$1792$$
$$1$$
$$19)1793(94$$
$$83$$
$$7 \text{ The Golden Number for that Year.}$$

EXAMPLE

EXAMPLE III.

What will be the Golden Number for the
Year 1766?

$$
\begin{array}{r}
1766 \\
1 \\
\hline
19)1767(93 \\
\cdot 57 \\
\hline
\end{array}
$$

In this laſt Example nothing remaining, the
Golden Number, according to the Rule, will
be 19.

Note, That the Golden Number is the
ſame in the *Julian*, as in the *Gregorian* Calendar.

CHAP. IV.

Of the EPACTS, *according to the* Julian
Calendar.

THE Solar Year containing 365 Days
5 Hours 48' 54" 41''' 27'''' 31''''',
and between one Conjunction of the Sun and
Moon, and another is 29 Days 12 Hours 44'
06", which multiplied by 12, gives 354 Days
08 Hours 49' 12" for the length of the Lunar
Year; which taken from the Solar Year, leaves 10
Days 20 Hours 59' 42" 41''' 27'''' 31''''. But to
avoid Fractions in Practice, the Epact is called

11, which you see is too much by 3 Hours 00′ 17″ 18‴ 32⁗ 29‴‴.

The RULE.

Multiply the Golden Number by 11, and divide the Product by 30, the Remainder is the Epact for the Year proposed.

EXAMPLE I.

What was the Epact for the Year 1748?

$$1748$$
$$1$$
———
$$19)1749(92$$
———
$$39$$
——

1 The Golden Number
11 Multiplied by
——

The Epact 11

In this Example, because 11 cannot be divided by 30, therefore the Epact is 11.

EXAMPLE

EXAMPLE II.

What was the Epact for the Year 1738 ?

$$1738$$
$$1$$
$$\overline{}$$

$$19)1739(91$$

$$.29$$

The Golden Number 10
Multiplied by 11

$$30)110(3$$

The Epact 20

CHAP. V.

Of the Gregorian EPACT.

THE Synodical Month, or the Space of Time contained between the Moon's parting from the Sun, at a Conjunction, and returning to him again, is 29 Days 12 Hours 44 Minutes and 6 Seconds, consequently 235 Lunations are made in 6939 Days 16 Hours 43 Minutes 30 Seconds; and 19 *Julian* Years are 6938 Days 18 Hours, and consequently, the New Moons, after 19 *Julian* Years, will not return to the same Hour of the Day, but will happen 1 Hour 16 Min. 30 Sec. sooner; which in the Space of 357 and $\frac{2}{3}$ Years, nearly; but,

according

according to some Authors, it will be but 310 Years, amounting to 1 entire Day, because they make the Length of the Lunar Synodical Month consist of 29 Days 12 Hours 44 Min. 3 Sec. Therefore 235 Lunations are made in 6939 Days 16 Hours 31 Min. 45 Sec. which are less than 19 *Julian* Years by 1 Hour 28 Min. 15 Sec. nearly agreeing with what the noble Earl of *Macclesfield* deliver'd in his Speech before the House of Peers, that noble Earl making the Anticipation in 19 Years to be 1 Hour 28 Min. 3 Sec. 30 Thirds, which in 310.7 Years, amounts to one entire Day.

And now because the New Moons do not return at the same Time of the Day, but 1 Hour 28' 03" 30''' sooner than they did 19 Years before; and that in 310 7 Years they will anticipate one Day, which proves that the Epact itself varies one Day in 310 7 Years, so that since the General Council of *Nice*, which was in the Year 325, the New Moons have antici-pated between 4 and 5 Days, and consequent-ly the Epacts should have decreased in the same Proportion, as the New Moons antici-pated, in order to find the Time of the New and Full Moons by the Epacts ; but before we can find the Epacts according to the *Gregorian* Calendar, we must find how many Days the *Gregorian* Stile has gained of the *Julian*, which how to find use this

R u l e I.

Reject two Figures or Cyphers, to the Right Hand, and divide the remaining Figures or Cyphers, consisting of entire Hundred Years by 4, reject the Remainder, and add 2 to the Quotient, this Sum substracted from the entire

C

Hun-

Hundred Years, leaves the Number of Days that the *Gregorian* Stile has gained of the *Julian*.

EXAMPLE I.

In the Year 3500, I would know how many Days the *Gregorian* Stile will have gained of the *Julian*.

4)35 The entire Hundred Years

The Quotient 8

Add 2

Sub. 10

25

Answ. The *Gregorian* will have gained of the *Julian* in that Year 25 Days.

EXAMPLE II.

In the Year 11752, I would know many Days the *Gregorian* will have gained of the *Julian* Stile?

4) 117 the entire Hundred Years

The Quotient 29
Add 2

Subtract 31

86 Days

Answ. The *Gregorian* will have gained of the *Julian* 86 Days; by which is plainly seen the Error of the *Julian* Stile.

To

To find the Gregorian *Epact.*

The RULE. II.

1ft. Find the *Julian* Epact, and then fubftract the Number of Days that the *Gregorian* Stile has gained of the *Julian,* from the *Julian* Epact, and the Remainder will be the *Gregorian* Epact, but if Subftraction cannot be made, you muft add 30, as often as needful.

EXAMPLE I.

I would find the *Gregorian* Epact for the Year 1753.

According to the laft Chap. I find the *Julian* Epact to be 6, and by the firft Rule in this Chap. I find that the *Gregorian* Stile is 11 Days before the *Julian,* then

$$
\begin{array}{lr}
\text{The } Julian \text{ Epact} & 6 \\
\text{Add} & 30 \\
\hline
\text{Sum} & 36 \\
\text{Subftract} & 11 \\
\hline
\text{The } Gregorian \text{ Epact} & 25 \\
\end{array}
$$

EXAMPLE II.

To find the *Gregorian* Epact for the Year 1786.

The *Julian* Epact for that Year will be 11, from which fubftract 11, the Number of Days that the *Gregorian* Stile has gained of the *Julian,* proves that that Year will have no Epact.

It was obferv'd before in this Chap. that the Epacts fhould be decreafed in Proportion to the

Anti-

Anticipation of the Moon, therefore the Rule already deliver'd will not hold good any longer than the Year 1799, but by the help of the following Table, the Epacts may be calculated for ever, and consequently the Moon's Age found from them will agree very near with the Truth.

No.	Years of our Lord	No to be fub	No	Years of our Lord.	No. to be fub.	No.	Years of our Lord.	No. to be fub.
1	1600	10	25	4000	20	49	6400	0
2	1700	11	26	4100	21	50	6500	1
3	1800	11	27	4200	22	51	6600	2
4	1900	12	28	4300	22	52	6700	3
5	2000	12	29	4400	22	53	6800	2
6	2100	12	30	4500	23	54	6900	3
7	2200	13	31	4600	23	55	7000	4
8	2300	14	32	4700	24	56	7100	4
9	2400	13	33	4800	24	57	7200	4
10	2500	14	34	4900	24	58	7300	5
11	2600	15	35	5000	25	59	7400	5
12	2700	15	36	5100	26	60	7500	6
13	2800	15	37	5200	25	61	7600	6
14	2900	16	38	5300	26	62	7700	6
15	3000	16	39	5400	27	63	7800	7
16	3100	17	40	5500	27	64	7900	8
17	3200	17	41	5600	27	65	8000	7
18	3300	17	42	5700	28	66	8100	8
19	3400	18	43	5800	28	67	8200	9
20	3500	19	44	5900	29	68	8300	9
21	3600	18	45	6000	29	69	8400	9
22	3700	19	46	6100	29	1	8500	10
23	3800	20	47	6200	0	2	8600	11
24	3900	20	48	6300	1	3	8700	11

This

This Table is composed of a Period 6900 Years which is numbred in the 1st Column of the Table from 1 to 69, the second Column contains the entire hundred Years, from 1600 to the Year 8700, and the third Column contains the Number that must be substracted from the *Julian* Epact, in order to find the *Gregorian*; this Table will be of great Use in order to find the mean Lunations for ever, and may be made perpetual by the following

RULE III.

Add to the entire Hundred Years the Number 54 and if the Sum exceeds 69, divide it by 69, and the Remainder will be the Number of the Period, but if the Sum is equal to, or less than 69, the Number of the Period is given by adding 54 to the Hundred Years.

EXAMPLE I.

I would know the Epact for the Year 325, the Year that the General Council of *Nice* was holden.

I find the Golden Number for that Year to be 3, the Epact 3 according to the *Julian* Calendar.

The Hundred Years   3
Add   54
—
The Number of the Period   57

With which I enter the 1st Column of the Table, and against it in the 3d Column stands 4, the Number to be substracted from the *Julian* Epact.

The

The *Julian* Epact   3
Add   30

Sum   33
Subſtract the Number of the } 4
Period
The Epact   29

EXAMPLE II.

What will be the Epact for the Year of our Lord 2104.

19)2104(110

20

The Golden Number   14
11

3|0)15|4(5

The *Julian* Epact   4
Add   30

The Sum   34
The Number of the } 12
Period ſubſtract
The Epact   22

By this Method of finding the Epacts, *Eaſter* Day, and all Things thereon depending, may for ever be found, according to the Method propoſed for correcting the Calendar.

CHAP.

CHAP. VI.

Of the Julian *Dominical Letter.*

THE Year is divided into 52 Weeks, of 7 Days each, and one Day over, by means of the first seven Letters of the Alphabet A, B, C, D, E, F, G, perpetually recurring throughout the Year. A stands against the 1st of *January*, B against the 2, and so on to *December* the 31st, which has A joined to it. The Letter which stands against all the Sundays of the Year, is called the Dominical or Sunday Letter for that Year. If *January* the 1st be *Sunday*, A is the Dominical Letter, which stands against every *Sunday* throughout the Year, except it be Leap-Year, for then the Dominical Letter changes at the End of *February*, moving a Letter backwards, so that G will be the *Sunday* Letter during the Remainder of the Year; for the Dominical Letter always shifts backwards, as from A to G, from G to F, and from F to E. If E be the Dominical Letter this Year, D will be the Dominical Letter for the next; to find the Dominical Letter for any Year, use this

R u l e.

Divide the Year, its 4th Part and 4 by 7, the Remainder subtract from 7, gives you the Number of the Letter, as here is set down.

A, B, C, D, E, F, G.

1, 2, 3, 4, 5, 6, 7.

Note,

Note, If after you divide by 7, nothing remain, the Dominical Letter is then G.

EXAMPLE I.

What is the Dominical Letter for the Year
1751?

$$4)1751$$
$$437$$
$$4$$

$$7)2192(7$$

$$313\text{-}1$$

$$6$$

The Number of the Dominical Letter.

The Number 6, according to the Rule, anfwers to F, fo that F is the Dominical Letter for
the Year.

EXAMPLE II.

What was the Dominical Letter for the
Year 1748?

$$4)1748$$
$$437$$
$$4$$

$$7)2189(7$$

$$312\text{-}5$$

$$2$$

The Number of the Dominical Letter.

Which, according to the Rule, anfwers
to B.

By

By the Dominical Letter, you may compute on what Day of the Week any Day of the Month will fall throughout the Year, by this

RULE.

1	2	3	4	5	6

At *Dover* Dwells *George Brown* Esquire,

7	8	9	10	11	12

Good *Christopher Finch*, And *David Frier*,

Where the twelve Words answers to the twelve Months. The first Letter of each Word stands in the Calendar against the first Day of the corresponding Month, as A against *January* the 1st, D against *February* the 1st, &c.

EXAMPLE I.

In the Year 1748, B was the Dominical Letter, I would know on what Day of the Week *June* the 24th was that Year.

E stands against *June* the 1st, *per* Rule; remember that the 1st, 8th, 15th, 22d, 29th, is the same Day of the Week in each Month. Now if B be *Sunday*, E is *Wednesday*, therefore *June* the 22d is *Wednesday*, consequently the 24th was of a *Friday*.

EXAMPLE II.

Suppose *Christmas* Day this Year 1751, I would know what Day of the Week it will fall on.

F is the Dominical Letter for this Year, and F stands against *December* the 1st, the 22d must be of a *Sunday*, and the 25th of *Wednesday*, *Christmas* Day.

D   CHAP.

CHAP. VII.

Of the Gregorian Dominical Letter.

THE Years following according to the *Gregorian* Calendar, are Years of 365 Days, *viz.* 1800, 1900, 2100, 2200, 2300, &c. and for thofe Years there is but one Dominical Letter, which Years, according to the *Julian* Calendar, would have two, which muft change the Courfe of the Dominical Letters quite different from the *Julian*. To find the *Gregorian* Dominical Letter, ufe the following

RULE.

Divide the Year and its 4th Part by 7, the Remainder fubtracted from 7 gives the Dominical Letter as in the *Julian* Calendar.

A, B, C, D, E, F, G.
1, 2, 3, 4, 5, 6, 7.

EXAMPLE I.

I would know the Dominical Letter for the Year 1754?

$$4)1754$$
$$438.2$$

$$7)2192(7$$

$$313 \quad 1$$

$$6$$

The Number of the Dominical Letter.

The

The Number 6, according to the Rule, gives the Dominical Letter F.

EXAMPLE II.

What will be the Dominical for the Year 1764 ?

$$4)1764$$
$$441$$

$$7)2205 \quad 7$$

$$315 \quad 0$$

The No. of the Letter 7   Anfwers to G.

This Method of finding the Dominical Letter, will only hold good for this Century ; the Dominical Letter then changing its Courfe, and then a Number muft be added to the Year, and its 4th, in order to find the Dominical Letters for ever, for which Purpofe take this

RULE.

Reject the Figures or Cyphers, to the Place of Hundreds. Divide the remaining Figures or Cyphers, by 4 , from this Quotient fubtract 1, and this Number fubtracted from the Hundred Years, and then this laft Remainder taken from the leaft Number of Sevens poffible, leaves a Number which muft be added to the Year and its 4th, in order to find the Dominical Letter according to the *Gregorian* Calendar.

What

Example I.

What will be the Dominical Letter for the Year 1842 ?

```
4)18(4  The  Quotient
  3 1  Subtract
  ───────
  15 3
  21
  ──
```

The No. to be added 6

```
  4)1842
    460
      6
  ─────────
  7)2308.7
    329.5
  ─────────
```

The No. of the Letter 2 Anfwers to B.

What will be the Dominical Letter for the Year 1947 ?

```
4)19(  4
  3    1
  ───────
  16   3
  21
  ──
```

The No. to be added 5

```
  4)1947
    486
      5
  ─────────
  7)2438 7
  ─────────
    348 2
  ─────────
```

The No. of the Letter 5 Anfwers to F

Or the *Gregorian* Dominical Letter may be found by subtracting the Number of Days that the *Gregorian* Stile has gained of the *Julian*, before you divide by 7, in proceeding to find the *Julian* Dominical Letter.

The Number of Days that the *Gregorian* Stile has gained of the *Julian*, may be found by the 1ft Rule of the 5th Chapter, the two laft Examples work'd by this Rule.

```
4)18(4
   6 2
   ─────
   12 6
   ─────
4)1842
   460
     4
   ─────
  2306
    12
   ─────
7)2294 7
   327 5
   ─────
      2
```

The Number of the Dominical Letter, as before, anfwers to B.

EXAMPLE II.

4)19(4
 6 2

___

13 6

___

4)1947
 486
   4

___

2437
Sub. 13

___

7)2424 7
  346 2

___

Number of the Letter 5 anſwers to E.

CHAP. VIII.

Of Eaſter *Day, according to the* Julian *Calendar.*

BY a too ſtrict Adherence to the *Julian* Year, and that too much applauded erroneous Lunar Cycle, invented by *Meton* the *Athenian,* 400 Years before our Saviour's Incarnation, and unluckily introduced into the Chriſtian Calendar 8 or 9 Hundred Years after, *Eaſter* fails in theſe Times, at leaſt thrice in 21 Years of being obſerved, as the Rule in the Common-Prayer-Book hath eſtabliſhed it, for the Rule ſays, " *Eaſter* Day (on which the reſt
" depends)

" depends) is always the firſt *Sunday* after the
" firſt Full Moon which happens next after the
" 21ſt Day of *March*, and if the Full Moon
" happens on a *Sunday*, *Eaſter* Day is the *Sunday*
" after." This Grand Feſtival is often celebrated
on the 22d of *March*, quite contradictory to the
foregoing Rule.

But this Error is ſtill increaſed according to the
Rule firſt eſtabliſhed by the General Council of
Nice, which runs thus : Firſt, That *Eaſter* ſhould
every where be begun to be obſerved on the firſt
Day of the Week, that is *Sunday*. Secondly,
That it ſhould be on the *Sunday* that ſhould follow
next after the 14th of the Moon that ſhould
happen next after the Vernal Equinox. And,
Thirdly, That it ſhould be referred to the Biſhop
of *Alexandria*, to calculate every Year on what
Day, according to theſe Rules, the ſaid Feſtival
ſhould begin. When it's very well known in
theſe Times that the 14th of the Moon, or the
Full Moon, as they called it, happens very often
between the 9th or 10th of *March*, and the 21ſt
Day of the ſaid Month, which contradicts the
aforeſaid Canons, every time it ſo happens. But
it's to be hoped theſe Difficulties will be removed
ſoon ; but till they are make uſe of this

R U L E.

Find the Epact for the Year propoſed, and if
it is leſs than 28 or 29, ſubtract it from 47 ; but
if be 28 or 29, ſubtract it from 77, the Remainder is the Day of the Month in *March* or
April, or *Eaſter* Limit for that Year, which if
it be leſs than 31, look in the Month of *March*,
and count on from that Day or Limit, till you
come to the *Sunday* Letter for that Year, for
that is *Eaſter* Day. But if the Limit exceeds

31, subtract 31 from it, and count in *April* for the Day or Limit, until your reckoning end àt the Dominical Letter for that Year; and that gives you *Easter* Day in *April*. Or having the Dominical Letter for any given Year, number it as is directed Chapter VI. and add 4 to it always. This Sum take from the Limit; what remains, you must subtract from the nearest Sum of Sevens; and this Remainder you must add to *Easter* Limit, gives *Easter* Day in *March*, if less than 32, or in *April* if more.

EXAMPLE I.

If the given Year is 1752, on what Day will *Easter* fall?

The Dominical Letter, according to Chapter VI. will be D, and the Epact 25, according to Chap. IV.

$$
\begin{array}{r}
\text{From } 47 \\
\text{Sub. Epact. } 25 \\
\hline
\end{array}
$$

$$
\begin{array}{r}
\textit{Easter} \text{ Limit } 22 \\
\text{Sum of the Letter } + 4. \ 8 \\
\hline
\end{array}
$$

$$
\begin{array}{r}
14 \\
\text{Nearest Sum of } 7\text{s} - 21 \\
\hline
\end{array}
$$

$$
\begin{array}{r}
7 \ \text{Add to Limit } 22 \\
7 \\
\hline
\end{array}
$$

Easter Day, *March* 29

EXAMPLE II.

What Day of the Month was *Easter* Day, 1740?

The Epact 12.
The Dominical Letter E.

From 47
Sub. Epact 12
———
Easter Limit 35
Sum of the Letter + 4 = 9
———
26
Nearest Sum of 7 s. 28
——
2 Add to Limit 35
2
——
37
March 31
Easter Day, *April* 6.

All the rest of the moveable Feasts being dependant on *Easter*, may very soon be found, for *Shrove-Sunday* is seven Weeks before *Easter*, and *Whit-Sunday* seven Weeks after, *Ascension* Day forty Days after, and *Trinity Sunday* eight Weeks after *Easter* Day, &c.

E   CHAP.

CHAP. IX.

Of Easter *Day, according to the* Gregorian *Calendar.*

IT was obſerved in the laſt Chapter, that the Feaſt of *Eaſter* was very often obſerved erroneouſly, according to the *Julian* Calendar ; but, according to the *Gregorian* Calendar, *Eaſter* Day will always be obſerved, as it was eſtabliſhed by the General Council of *Nice, Anno 325, viz.* The firſt *Sunday* after the firſt Full Moon, that happens upon or next after the Day of the Vernal Equinox ; and if the Full Moon happen on a *Sunday, Eaſter* Day will always be the *Sunday* after. So that *Eaſter* Full Moon will always happen between the 21ſt Day of *March,* and the 18th of *April,* both Days incluſive. The Time of the Vernal Equinox being fixed by the *Gregorian* Calendar to the 21ſt Day of *March,* according to the aforeſaid Eſtabliſhment, *Eaſter* Day may always be found by the following

RULE.

Seek the Epact for the Year propoſed, and if it is leſs than 24, ſubtract it from 44, but if it exceeds 24, ſubtract it from 74 ; and if the Epact is 24, it muſt be taken from 73, and alſo if the Epact is 25, and the Golden between 12 and 19, both Numbers incluſive, the Epact, muſt be taken from 73, the Remainder will be *Eaſter* Limit, or the Day of the Paſchal Full Moon. If the Limit is leſs than 32, the Full Moon is in *March,* but if it exceeds 31, the Day of the Full Moon is in *April.* The *Sunday* after is *Eaſter* Day.

EXAMPLE

EXAMPLE I.

I would know *Easter* Day for the Year 1753?

$$1753$$
$$1$$

$$19)1754(\ 92$$

$$44$$

The Golden Number 6
Multiplied by 11

$$30)66(2$$

The *Julian* Epact   6
Add 30

$$36$$
Subtract 11

The *Gregorian* Epact 25

From 74
Sub. *Gregorian* Epact 25

Easter Limit 49
Sub. *March* 31

Easter Limit *April* 18

The Dominical Letter by Chap. VII. will be found G ; then add 4 to the Number of the Dominical Letter (as in Chap. VIII.) and subtract this Sum from *Easter* Limit, and the Re-

fidue

fidue from the neareft greater Sum of Sevens, this laft Remainder added to the Limit, gives *Eafter* Day.

The WORK.

Eafter Limit	49
Sum of the Letter and 4	11
	——
Remainder Sub.	38
Neareft Sum of Sevens	42
	——
4 Add to Limit	49
	4
	——
Sum	53
March	31
	——
Eafter Day *April*	22

Eafter Day according to the *Julian* Calendar, fhould be the 11th of *April.*

EXAMPLE II.

What Day of the Month will *Eafter* Day happen on for the Year 1754?

Find by Chap. 3, the Golden Number	7
Find by Chap. 5, the Epact ———	6
And by Chap. 7, the Dominical Letter	F

then

```
            From    44
        Sub. Epaƈt.   6
                     ──
         Remains    38
  Sum, Letter and 4  10
                     ──
        Rem. Sub.   28
  Neareſt Sum of Sevens 35
                     ──
              7   Add to Limit  38
                                 7
                                ──
                        Sum    45
                      March    31
                                ──
```

Eaſter Day *April* 14

Eaſter Day found by the *Julian* Calendar will be the 3d of *April*.

EXAMPLE III.

What Day of the Month will *Eaſter* Day fall on in the Year 3203?

```
      The Year    3203
         Add         1
                   ────
           19)3204(168
                ────
              130
              ────
              164
              ────
  The Golden Number   12
      Multiplied by   11
                     ────
         3|0)13|2(4   The Quotient.
                ────
  The Julian Epaƈt   12
```

I

I find by the Table Chap. 8. Page 12, that 17 is the Number to be subtracted from the *Julian* Epact, then

$$
\begin{array}{lr}
\text{The Epact } \textit{Julian} & 12 \\
\text{Add} & 30 \\
\hline
& 42 \\
\text{Sub. the Number in the Table} & 17 \\
\hline
\text{The Epact } \textit{Gregorian} & 25 \\
\end{array}
$$

Find how many Days the *Gregorian* Stile has gained of the *Julian*, by Chap. 5, Rule 1.

$$
\begin{array}{lr}
4)32 & \text{The entire Hundred} \\
\hline
& \quad\quad\text{Years.}
\end{array}
$$

$$
\begin{array}{lr}
\text{The Quotient} & 8 \\
\text{Add} & 2 \\
\hline
\text{Subtract} & 10 \\
\hline
\end{array}
$$

The *Gregorian* Stile will have gained of the *Julian* } 22

Now to find the Dominical Letter, proceed

$$
\begin{array}{r}
4)3203 \\
8\text{o}0 \\
4 \\
\hline
4007 \\
\end{array}
$$

Number of Days found 22

$$
7)3985(7
$$

$$
569\text{---}2
$$

The Number of the Dominical Letter 5 answers to E.

According

According to the Rule the Epact muſt be taken from 73 (becauſe the Epact is 25 and the Golden Number 12) in order to find *Eaſter* Limit, then

To find Eaſter *Day.*

From	73
Sub. Epact.	25
	——
Eaſter Limit	48
Sum of the Letter and 4 =	9
Rem. Sub.	39
Neareſt Sum of Sevens	42
	——

3	Add to Limit	48
		3
		——
	Sum	51
	March	31
		——
	April the	20

So that *Eaſter* Day according to the *Gregorian* Calendar will happen on the 20th of *April.* I obſerve in this Queſtion that the Vernal Equinox in that Year will have gone back 11 Days more, ſo that the Vernal Equinox that Year will happen the 27th of *February,* (if the *Julian* Stile continue in Uſe ſo long) and *Eaſter* Day in thoſe Times will not happen once in three Years according to its firſt Eſtabliſhment by the General Council of *Nice.*

But it may be aſked by ſome People, why *Eaſter* ſhould be a moveable Feaſt any more than the Deaths of the Apoſtles, or other Feaſt and Faſt Days obſerved by the Church of *England?*

To

To which I anſwer, 1ſt. That there might be ſome Analogy, or Correſpondency between the Jewiſh * and Chriſtian *Paſcha*, or *Eaſter*, but ſo, that the Jewiſh Solemnity might at no Time concur with the Chriſtian Memorial of the Reſurrection of *Chriſt*. 2dly. That at no Time an Eclipſe of the Sun ſhould be ſeen at the Feaſt of *Eaſter*, as that, which was miraculous at the Death of *Chriſt*, and, contrary to the Courſe of Nature, happening at the Full Moon, left it might give Occaſion to the *Jews* and *Infidels* to calumniate the *Chriſtians*.

CHAP. X.

Of the Moon's Age.

THE Age of the Moon found by the Epacts is near the Truth, according to the Moon's middle Motion, and may be found by the following

RULE.

Add to the Epact for the given Year the Day of the Month, and the Number of the Months as here is ſet down, and if the Sum is under 30, that is, the Moon's Age, but if it exceeds 30, caſt away 30, and the Remainder is the Moon's Age. The Months muſt be numbered thus,

0	2	1	2	3	4
January,	*February,*	*March,*	*April,*	*May,*	*June,*
5	6	8	8	10	
July,	*Auguſt,*	*September,*	*October,*	*November,*	
10					
December.					

* *Exodus* the xii and xiii Chapters, *Luke* the xxii, *Matthew* the xxvi, *Mark* the xiv

Note,

Note, You muſt make uſe of the Epact for the Stile that you would find the Moon's Age for.

EXAMPLE I.

How old will the Moon be the 20th of *May,* 1753 ? according to the *Gregorian* Stile.

Find the Epact by Chap. V. which is 25.

The Epact 25
The Number of the Month 3
The Day of the Month 20
————
48
30
————
The Moon's Age 18 Days
————

The Day of the New Moon is gained by adding the Number of the Month, and the Epact together, and ſubtract the Sum from 30; but if the Sum exceeds 30, ſubtract it from 59, and the Remainder is the Day of the New Moon, according to her middle Motion, and the Day of the Full Moon is gained by ſubſtracting the above-mentioned Sum from 15 , but when Subſtraction cannot be made, borrow 30 Days, and the Remainder will give you the Day of the Full Moon, according to her mean Motion.

F

Ex-

EXAMPLE II.

I would know the Day of, the Full Moon for the Month of *December*, 1753.

The Epact as before 25
The Num. of the Month 10
___

Take 35
___

30
15
___

From 45
Answ. Full Moon the 10 Day of *December*.

EXAMPLE III.

I would know the Day of the New Moon for the Month of *August*, 1753?

The Epact 25
Number of the Month 6
___

31
59
___

New Moon the 28 Day of *August*.

EXAMPLE

E X A M P L E IV.

I would know the Moon's Age for the 5th Day of *September*, 1754.

Find the Epact by Chap. V. which is 6.

The Epact	6
The Number of the Month	8
The Day of the Month	5

The Moon's Age   19 Days

How old will the Moon be *July* 6, *Anno* 3504?

$$3504$$
$$1$$

$$19)3505(184$$
$$160$$

$$85$$

The Golden No.	9
Multiplied by	11

$$3|0)9|9(3$$

The *Julian* Epact   9

I find by the Table, Chap. V. Page 12. that 19 is the Number to be fubtracted from the *Julian* Epact, in order to find the *Gregorian* Epact.

     The

The *Julian* Epact   9
Add   30

The Sum   39
The Number ſub.   19

The *Gregorian* Epact   20

The Epact   20
The Number of the Month   5
The Day of the Month   6

From 31

Sub. 30

The Age of the Moon 1 Day.

In all theſe Examples the Moon's Age was found for the *Gregorian* Stile; but if you would find it for the *Julian*, you muſt make uſe of the *Julian* Epact.

C H A P. XI.

Of the Moon's Southing.

THE Moon's Southing, is the Time of her coming to, or upon the Meridian; which, from the New Moon to her Full, is after Noon, but from the Full to the Change, is before Noon, in finding which uſe this

RULE.

R u l e.

Multiply the Moon's Age by 4, and divide the Product by 5, the Quotient is Hours, and the Remainder is so many 12 Minutes of an Hour.

E x a m p l e I.

I would find the Time of the Moon's coming to the South the 17th of *May*, 1753.

25 The Epact found by Chap. V.

The Epact	25
The Number of the Month	3
The Day of the Month	17
	45
	30
The Moon's Age	15
Multiplied by	4

5)60(12 Hours. The Time of the Moon's coming to the South.

The Moon will come to the South, or be upon the Meridian, at Twelve o'Clock at Night.

Example

EXAMPLE II.

I would know the Time of the Moon's coming to the South, *Anno* 1805, *March* the 25th.

First find the Epact.

The Year   1805
Add   1
———
19)1806(94
———
96
—
The Golden Number 20
Multiplied by   11
3|0)22|0(7
———
The *Julian* Epact   10
———

I find by the Table Chap. V. Page 12, that 11 is the Number, to be subtracted from the *Julian* Epact, in order to find the *Gregorian* Epact

The *Julian* Epact	10
Add	30
	—
The Sum	40
Subtract	11
	—
The *Gregorian* Epact	29

The Epact *Gregorian*   29
The Number of the Month   1
The Day of the Month   25
—

The

The Sum	55
Subtract	30
The Moon's Age	25
Subtract	15
Days after the Full	10
Multiplied by	4

$$5)40($$

The Time of the Moon's } 8 Hours.
fouthing

Becaufe the Moon is paft the Full, therefore the Moon comes to the South the 26th Day, at 8 o'Clock in the Morning, or the 25th Day, at 12 Min. after 7 in the Morning.

EXAMPLE III.

To find the Time of the Moon's coming to the South for the Year 3427, *June* the 15th.

The Year 3427
Add   1

$$19)3428(180$$

152

The Golden Number   8
Multiplied by   11

$$3|0)8|8|2$$

The *Julian* Epact   28

I find

I find in the Table, Chap. 5. Page 12, that 18 is the Number to be Subtracted from the *Julian* Epact, in order to find the *Gregorian* Epact, then

The *Julian* Epact	28
Subtract the No. found in the Table	18
The *Gregorian* Epact	10
Add the Number of the Month	4
Add the Day of the Month	15
The Moon's Age	29 Days
Subtract	15
Days after the Full	14
Days after the Full	14
Multiplied by	4
5)56	
	11 : 12

The Time of the Moon's coming to the South is 12 Min. after 11 o'Clock in the Morning.

Of the Time of High Water.

WHEN the Sun and Moon are in Conjunction, or Opposition, that is, at New or Full Moon, the Attraction of both these Bodies acting upon the Earth in the same Direction, or in the same Right Line, their Force is united to elevate the Waters, whereby are produced Spring Tides, and the highest Spring Tides are before the Vernal and after the autumnal Equinox.

When

When the Moon is in her Quadratures, her Attraction acts in one Direction, the Sun's in a quite contrary ; by which Means they correct or counteract one another, the Moon raising the Waters where the Sun depresses them, and *vice versa,* which produces Neap-Tides, and the weakest Neap-Tides happen, when the Sun is near the Tropics.

The Time of High Water may be found near enough for common Use by the following

RULE.

To the Moon's Southing, add the Point of the Compass making Full Sea (on the Full and Change Day) for the Place proposed, that Sum is the Time of High Water or Full Sea.

The Hours and Minutes answering to the Point of the Compass making Full Sea, may be had by Inspection from the following Table, for the following Places.

G

The

Subtract H M	The Names of PORTS.	Add H. M.
12 24	Portfmouth, Southampton, Queenborough, Ifle of Wight.	0 0
11 38	Rocheſter, Aberdeen, Winchelſea, and Fluſhing.	0 46
10 51	Downs, Gravefend, Scilly, Thanet, and Guernſey.	1 33
10 5	London, Dundee, St Andrews, Holy-Ifle, and Bell-Ifle.	2 19
9 19	Tinmouth, Hartlepool, and West Coaſt of Ireland	3 6
8 32	Bridlington-bay, Berwick, Flamborough, Rochel.	3 52
7 45	Scarborough, Mounts-bay, Kinfale, and Humber.	4 39
6 59	Newcaſtle, Falmouth, Dartmouth, Lizard.	5 25
6 12	Plymouth, Hull, Lynn, Foſdike, and Croſs-keys.	6 12
5 26	Weymouth, Lime, Briſtol, Boſton, St. Nicholas.	6 53
4 40	Milford-haven, Bridgewater, Land's-end, Portland.	7 45
3 53	Hague, Dublin, Peterport, Harflew, St. Magnus.	8 31
3 7	Pool, St. Helens, Cathneſs, Orkney, Ifle of Man.	9 18
2 20	The Needles, Layſtow, the North and South Forelands.	10 4
1 33	Yarmouth, Dover, Harwich, Cowes, and Calais-Road.	10 51
0 47	Rye, Sole-bay, Goore, and Margaret-Road.	11 37

The

The Use of the Table is very easy to understand; for if on any Day proposed you subtract the Hours and Minutes that stand in the Left Hand Column against any Port, from the Time of the Moon's Southing, or add those in the Right Hand Column, the Difference and Sum of those Numbers will be the Times of High Water at the Place required.

EXAMPLE I.

I would know the Time of High Water at *London* the 16th of *September*, 1753.

I find by Chap. V. the Epact for that Year, which is 25.

The Epact	25
The Number of the Month	8
The Day of the Month	16
	——
	49
Subtract	30
	——
The Moon's Age	19 Days
	4
	——
	5)76(
	——
	151:2

I subtract 10 H. 5 Min. the Left Hand tabular Number against *London*, from 15 H. 12 M. and the Difference is 5 H. 7 Min. Afternoon, the Time of High Water at *London* on that Day, then I add 2 H. 19 M the Right Hand tabular Number, to the said Time of her Southing, and the Sum is 17 H. 31 M. Afternoon, that is the 17th Day, at 31 M. after 5 in the Morning, for the next Time of High Water at *London.*

Ex-

EXAMPLE II.

I would know the Time of High-Water for *Gravefend* the 29th of *May*, 1946?

$$1946$$
$$\text{Add} \quad 1$$
$$\overline{}$$

$$19)1947(102$$

$$47$$

The Golden Number   9
Multiplied by   11

$$3|0)9|9($$

The *Julian* Epact   9
Add   30

39
Number in the Table fub.   12

The *Gregorian* Epact   27
The Number of the Month   3
The Day of the Month   29

59
Sub.   30

29
Sub.   15

Days after the Full   14
Multiplied by   4

$$5)56$$

Moon's South   11 : 12

Σ

I find in the Tide Table that 10 h. 51 min. is to be subftracted for *Gravefend*, and 1 h. 33 min. added.

The Moon's Southing   11 : 12
Sub.   10 : 51

High Water   0 : 21

High Water   12 : 45

So that the Times of High Water are 29 D. 12 H. 21 Min. or 21 Min. after 12 in the Morning the 30th Day, and the next Tide 45 Min. after 12 at Noon the 30th Day.

The Time of the Tides found as above, will be near enough for common Ufe, or you may make about 20 Min. Allowance, as is directed in the 1ft Part of this Chapter.

Note in the three laft Chapters, I have made ufe of the *Gregorian* Epacts, but, if you would find the Moon's Age, Moon's Southing, or the Time of High Water for the *Julian* Stile, you muft make Ufe of the *Julian* Epact.

CHAP. XIII.

Of the Calends, Nones, *and* Ides.

THE Calends are the firft Day of each Month. The Nones are the 7th Day of the four Months, *March, May, July,* and *October,* and the 5th Day of the other Months : And the Ides come 8 Days after the Nones, that is, on the 15th Day of *March, May, July,* and *October,* and the 13th of the other Months.

The

The other Days are counted backwards, still diminishing the Number; for the Days between the Calends, and the Nones of any Month, are denominated from the Nones; and so of the rest as you see in the Calendar.

C H A P. XIV.

Of the Roman Indiction.

THE Roman Indiction has no Connexion with the Celestial Motions, but because the Famous Period of 7980, called the *Julian* Period, is producted from it, I shall not pass it over in Silence.

The Roman Indiction is a Term of 15 Years, at the End of which they began their Computation with a continual Circulation; this Period was called Indiction as some will have it, because it serv'd to point out the Year of Payment of the Tax or Tribute to the Republick. To find it use this

R U L E.

Add three to the Year of our Lord, and divide the Sum by 15, and the Remainder is the Year of Indiction.

E X A M P L E I.

What was the Roman Indiction for the Year 1730.

1730

$$\text{Add} \begin{array}{r} 1730 \\ 3 \end{array}$$

$$15)1733(115$$

$$23$$

$$83$$

The Roman Indiction   8

EXAMPLE II.

What was the Roman Indiction for the Year 1740?

$$\text{Add} \begin{array}{r} 1740 \\ 3 \end{array}$$

$$15)1743(116$$

$$24$$

$$93$$

The Roman Indiction   3

CHAP. XV.

Of the Julian *Period.*

THE *Julian* Period is a Cycle of 7980 Years, produced by the Multiplication of three Cycles, *viz.* That of the Sun 28, of the Moon 19, and that of the Roman Indiction 15 Years, this was the Invention of *Julius Scaliger*, who fixed the Beginning of it 764 Years before the Creation;

Creation; so that at the Birth of *Christ* it was 4712. Therefore, if to the current Year of *Christ* you add 4713, the Sum will be the Year of the *Julian* Period; and from the Year of the *Julian* Period subtract 4713, there will remain the Year of the Christian *Æra*.

EXAMPLE I.

I would know the *Julian* Period for the Year 1753.

$$
\begin{array}{r}
1753 \\
\text{Add} \quad 4713 \\
\hline
\text{The } \textit{Julian} \text{ Period} \quad 6466
\end{array}
$$

EXAMPLE II.

What was the *Julian* Period for the Year 1604?

$$
\begin{array}{r}
1604 \\
\text{Add} \quad 4713 \\
\hline
\text{The } \textit{Julian} \text{ Period} \quad 6317
\end{array}
$$

EXAMPLE III.

I would know the Year of *Christ* when the *Julian* Period will be 7604.

$$
\begin{array}{r}
7604 \\
\text{Sub.} \quad 4713 \\
\hline
\text{The Year of } \textit{Christ} \quad 2891
\end{array}
$$

FINIS.

Printed in the USA
CPSIA information can be obtained
at www.ICGtesting.com
LVHW010041071123
763241LV00012B/390